Shiny and Soaring

What Am I?

by Joyce Markovics

Consultant: Eric Darton, Adjunct Faculty
New York University Urban Design and Architecture Studies Program
New York, New York

BEARPORT
PUBLISHING

New York, New York

Credits

Cover, © Alexander Prokopenko/Shutterstock and Grisha Bruev/Shutterstock; 2, © Vlad Lazarenko/CC BY-SA 4.0; TOC, © Michail Makarov/Shutterstock; 4–5, © Kev Llewellyn/Shutterstock; 6–7, © Monkey Business Images/Shutterstock; 8–9, © Vlad Lazarenko/CC BY-SA 4.0 and © Pakhnyushchy/Shutterstock; 10–11, © Richard Levine/Alamy; 12–13, © Mike Segar/Reuters; 14–15, © Drop of Light/Shutterstock; 16–17, © Mark Lennihan/Ap Images; 18–19, © Michail Makarov/Shutterstock; 20–21, © Michail Makarov/Shutterstock; 22, © Susan Candelario/Alamy; 23, © Dignity 100/Shutterstock; 24, © kropic1/Shutterstock.

Publisher: Kenn Goin
Senior Editor: Joyce Tavolacci
Creative Director: Spencer Brinker
Design: Debrah Kaiser
Photo Researcher: Thomas Persano

Library of Congress Cataloging-in-Publication Data in process at time of publication (2018)
Library of Congress Control Number: 2017039493
ISBN-13: 978-1-68402-483-4 (library binding)

For more information, write to Bearport Publishing Company, Inc., 45 West 21st Street, Suite 3B, New York, New York 10010. Printed in the United States of America.

10 9 8 7 6 5 4 3 2 1

Contents

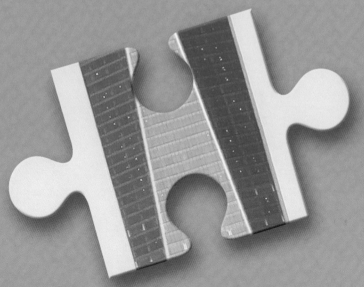

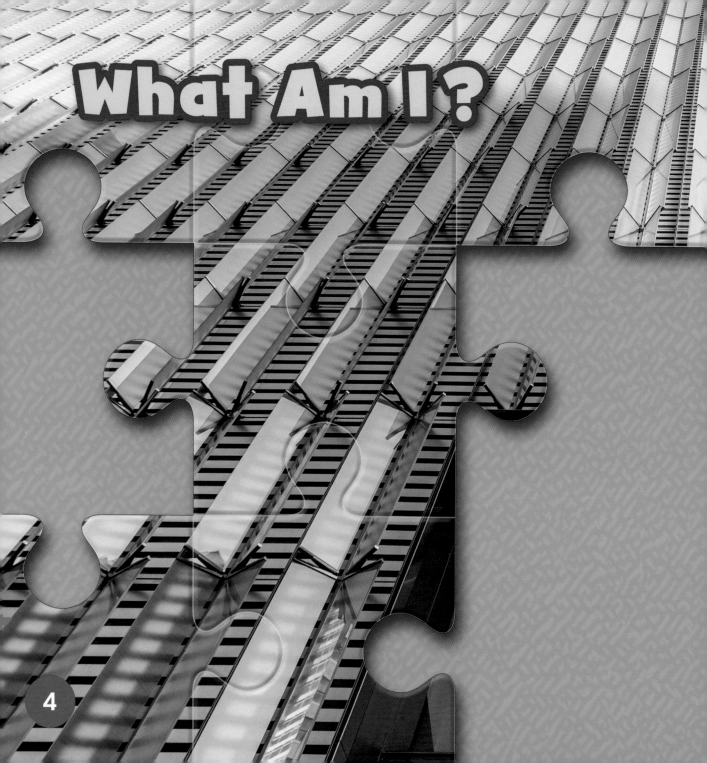

What Am I?

I am covered in shiny glass panels.

5

I have 104
floors.

6

Some contain
offices.

7

Look up! I have
a tall metal spire.

8

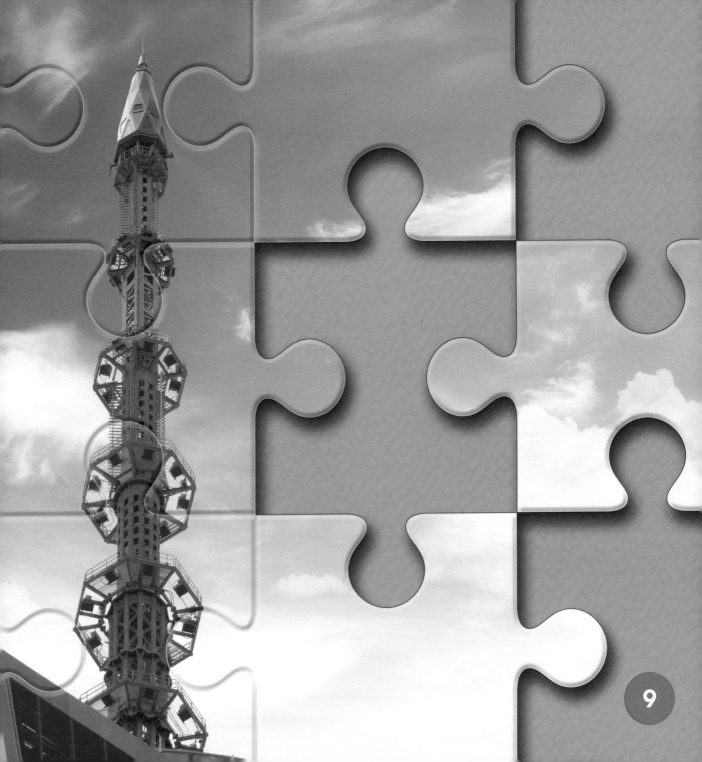

There is a huge lobby on my first floor.

I have 73 elevators.

13

Millions of people visit me each year.

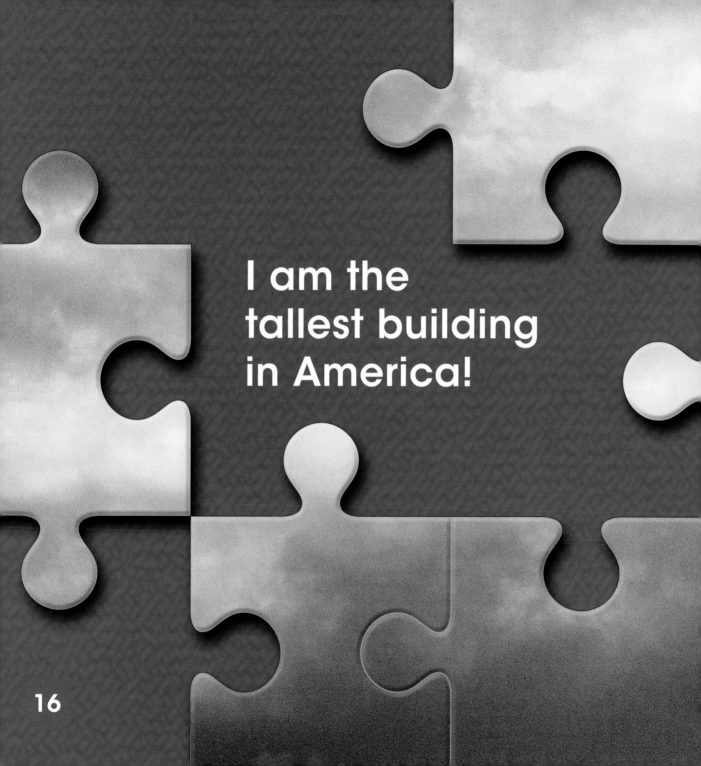

I am the
tallest building
in America!

16

17

What am I?

Let's find out!

19

I am One World Trade Center!

Fast Facts

One World Trade Center was built after the September 11, 2001, terrorist attacks. Its total height refers to the year 1776, when the Declaration of Independence was signed!

One World Trade Center

Total Height:	1,776 feet (541 m), including the spire
Weight:	48,000 tons (43,545 mt)
Number of Floors:	104
Amount of Office Space:	About 3 million square feet (278,709 sq. m)
Height of Lobby Ceiling:	55 feet (17 m)
Cool Fact:	The building has 12,774 glass panels on its outside.

Where Am I?

One World Trade Center is located in Lower Manhattan in New York City.

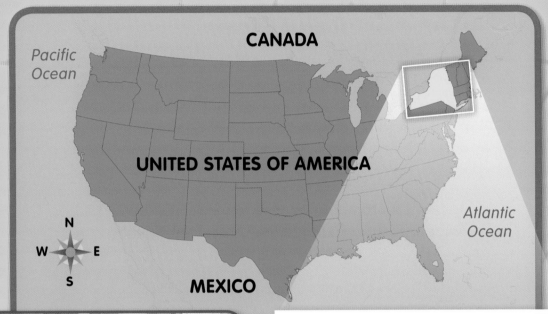

CANADA

Pacific Ocean

UNITED STATES OF AMERICA

Atlantic Ocean

N W E S

MEXICO

The 9/11 Memorial next to One World Trade Center

CANADA

NEW YORK

One World Trade Center

Index

Read More

Kaur, Ramandeep. *One World Trade Center (How Did They Build That?).* New York: Lightswitch Learning (2015).

Mansfield, Andy. *Pop-Up New York.* New York: Lonely Planet Kids (2016).

Learn More Online

To learn more about One World Trade Center, visit **www.bearportpublishing.com/AmericanPlacePuzzlers**

About the Author

Joyce Markovics is a proud New Yorker who lives in a very old house along the Hudson River.